How to Rock Your Bake Sale

I0429341

For Beginners, Go Getters, and Marketing Nuts!

Preface

Roxanne has been volunteering for bake sales for over 25 years and she is currently working on her Doctorate in Marketing at Capella University. She has volunteered with several non-profit organizations over the years for many quality causes. This book has been written to help those who volunteer their time and money to help others in need, see the potential for a little better return.

Table of Contents

Introduction

What is a bake sale all about? It is supposed to be about raising money for some kind of quality cause. Anything from cancer awareness, a school sports team, funeral coverage, sudden illness, fire damage, Multiple Sclerosis, and the list of great causes just goes on and on and on. Put your hand up, and start counting, I am certain you could name at least 5 quality causes that are near and dear to your heart.

So why do we do bake sales? In theory, it is a way to raise money for your quality cause. Bake sales are a great way to do this because everybody eats. It is easy to sell something to people that they need, and food is relatively simple to make, and can be cost effective. Most people make food, so asking them to make a little bit extra, to sit on a display table, and sell for some quality cause, is pretty easy to get behind. Asking a buyer to pass over a few dollars, for that quality cause for something tasty (usually sugary and sweet) tends to go well.

The trick, and probably why you are reading this book right now, is that you would like to maximize both your time and your effort. The output of an hour it took to bake those gooey delicious Chocolate Chip cookies, the $6 in ingredients it took to make them and the $1 in bags it took to get them ready to sell, needs to be worth the 5 hours you and your family spent standing at the table with others trying to bring in $300 for your cause. It's even possible that the amount of money spent to fill that table with baked goods was more than the money folks donated to buy them.

So where do we begin… At the beginning of course!

With the planning, the cause, the reason for the entire bake sale. People feel good about doing something good. They like to know that the money they are spending, and the time that they are donating is going to a quality reason. Throughout the chapters we will talk about the details and the finer points of holding a bake sale, but here… in the beginning… we will talk about your cause. Your need and your want, the reason for your bake sale, why it is so important that the individuals visiting your table understand what you are doing. In the 10 seconds it takes them to glance over your table, they should know why this is so important. Where the money is going to go after they hand it over into your open hands.

Chapter 1. Know Your Cause

Every person who is volunteering for your bake sale needs to know the basics of your cause. They need to know whom to point folks to for the bigger details, especially who can take charge of larger donations. At one school bake sale I asked what the money was being raised for, and the kids looked at me blankly. I headed over to one of the adults and asked my question again (its ok I thought, the kids are just helping). The adult directed me over to a teacher who said that the funds were being raised for art projects. I was perfectly ok with the answer, but this was not a complicated question. Any of the kids or parents could have handled it. It would have only taken the teacher a few seconds to make an artsy sign telling all visitors to the table what the funds were being raised for, and even less time to make sure that the kids and parents understood what to tell people.

You never know when you will run across a philanthropist who feels strongly about your cause and would throw a few hundred dollars at your situation. I have had that happen 3 times now at my bake sales. Someone walking past read our signs, and stepped up asking for a little more information. One volunteer was able to explain that the money raised would be used in their community and the individual gave a $100 donation. Another example I would share was going towards raising money for a special interest camp, which was in need of supplies. This donor gave us $200 which more than paid for several paddles and a life jacket.

So again I say, KNOW YOUR CAUSE! I also add to that, everyone working at the bake sale should KNOW YOUR CAUSE! Just like in any line of sales, it is a missed opportunity when you can't tell a potential investor what the money will support. You may have the greatest cause in the entire world, your cause could save the life of every baby, animal, cancer patient, homeless person, veteran, or pink striped unicorn, but if your volunteers can't answer the questions, then the people just don't know.

So make up cheat sheets if you need to for each volunteer to carry in his or her pocket. Take a few minutes to make cardboard, or cardstock displays for the table outlining the specific need of the day so that volunteers can just point to the displays, but ensure that they have a key person or contact number that people can call for more information. The more information that you have available to those visiting your booth, the more they will know about your cause. That being said, the information should take up no more than one foot by one foot of space on your table.

Consider having a separate table like one that you would use at the end of a couch for displaying all of your printed materials if you need more space. An end table with a nice tablecloth could provide an additional level to your display and a way to keep the food separate from the paperwork.

Also, higher tables such as standing tables can work well for this purpose. Even two sawhorses with a sheet of wood will work. Be sure to secure the wood to the sawhorses.

Chapter 2. Answering Questions

If you are raising money for any cause, there are going to be questions about where the money is going. If you never get asked that question, GREAT, but most folks, at one time or another, will. If you are a school group or a church, it is probably taken for granted that the monies are attached to a quality cause or a non-profit or not-for-profit type of organization. Other causes or organizations may have to work harder to prove that they are toeing the line or at the least, that they are actually using the monies to meet the efforts (causes) that they have identified.

We need to understand that communities can have different responses to individuals or groups fundraising in their areas. I have seen situations where individuals or families have sat at tables loaded with goods, and communities have shunned them; folks who for some reason did not have the support that they needed. Their communities turned their backs on those families needs for one reason or another and what could have been a successful bake sale…failed.

How do you prepare yourself for success? First you need to be open about your cause. Have as much information as possible available. If you are raising money for an individual, take the time to print out a single sheet of paper outlining the specific needs that the money is going towards. An example of this is an individual who was struggling with cancer and the family needed funds to help pay for premiums, so the family was raising money for that specific cause.

A great follow up to a successful fundraising event is to send a letter to the editor of the local newspaper outlining what the fundraiser was able to help with. If you had a website involved, or a Facebook, Google+, and/or Twitter page then make a posting there. Consider something like this: *"John and Sarah Smith would like to thank all of the folks in our community who made purchases at the bake sale on Saturday, it allowed us to purchase a couch and dining room table to replace those lost in the fire last month. The house is really starting to feel like a home again!"* Something so small really speaks to a community. If it is a funeral that you were fundraising for then consider, *"With the loving help of our community and their donations at our bake sale on Sunday, a significant portion of the Smith family's funeral expenses have been paid. We can not say thank you enough to this amazing and giving community."* Its important for people to know how they are helping, let them know that they are a part of the success.

If you received a particularly large donation from someone, then announce that as well. *"As well as thanking everyone who gave at our bake sale this weekend, we would like to give a special thank you to one anonymous donor who gave $200, the little league team appreciates your* *generous heart."* If you would like to mention those donors by name do that, but make sure you ask the person first.

If you are fundraising for an established organization you are required to obtain proper authorization from that organization. This could be in the form of an e-mail or letter from the organization confirming their permission for you to raise funds in their name. If possible a copy of this should be available at your bake sale. Then try to have brochures or fliers on hand specific to this organization. When possible have a representative from that organization on hand to answer specific questions. Posters and logos for an organization should be prominently displayed. The last thing anyone wants to have happen is for a group to be fundraising for a quality cause and this get their integrity is questioned because they don't have the right permissions in place to be doing that fundraising.

The Big Questions

There is a general list of questions that you should be prepared to answer. Feel free to copy this list below onto a handout and provide to your volunteers:

- Who benefits from the money raised?
- What is the money being raised to do?
- What is the money being spent on?
- Where is the group or individual located that will receive the money?
- Where is the money being spent?

- When is the money going to be used (month/day/year)?
- Why is this important to our buyers?
- Why is this important to me as the volunteer?
- How can I help in the future, or is there anything else I can do to help your group?
- * If you are a membership type of organization you need to consider this question... How can the person donating join?

The first part of preparing for your bake sale is one of the most important parts... knowing your cause. Now comes the harder part, getting other individuals to rally behind your cause and getting them to bake delicious bites of food to sell at your event.

Chapter 3. The Basics

The most basic of basics

What makes a successful bake sale? There are 5 key things that will ensure that your bake sale is very successful. The rest of the book breaks each of these steps into a chapter and the final chapter is for the marketing nut. This person wants to dig deep into the logic behind sales and see how things tick. This person, who like me, wants to know the reason why one group can sit outside of the super center for 4 hours and make $3,000 and the next group sits outside the super center for 9 hours and makes $200.

The Keys

1. The Big Picture
2. The Volunteers
3. The Location
4. The Display
5. Food
6. Money

Key 1. You are a big picture

You are a picture, from the second a person looks in your direction they need to know that they are approaching a bake sale. What are some of the things that will help that happen:

- Sign – Beautiful sign! It doesn't need to be a professional sign, or even a computer printed sign. What it does need to be is easy to read and have the words BAKE SALE printed on it in large lettering. Any other information that you place on the sign other than the words bake sale, should be smaller and a different color. If you would like to make the words BAKE SALE in bright colors, try to keep each word the same color so that it is easier to read. Keeping in mind that dark colors on a light background or light colors on a dark background are easiest for people to see.
- Supporting Display and Mascots – A tent with your sign hung, or just flagpoles with your BAKE SALE sign. Some sort of sign with lettering telling them that they are approaching a bake sale and the name of the group hosting the bake sale. Additional display items to consider: Supporting display items for your group like paintings, motorcycles, antique cars, rehabilitation equipment, etc… All of these types of items that

represent your group, for example a group like the Combat Veterans Motorcycle Association might park one of the members bikes next to their bake sale table to attract attention.

- Tables – Make sure they aren't wobbly, and consider using boxes or upside down bowls to make raised levels to elevate baked goods to see the goods in the back more easily. Try to use tablecloths of solid colors so that the tablecloth isn't competing with the items sitting on it. Use attractive bowls, baskets and plastic bins to separate the baked goods on the table and use little stands to identify items. This gives the feeling of being in store. Labels can be made with card stock by folding a smaller piece into a box and writing on the top and front side, then taping the edges together. Also tape the cardstock to the table or the container with the baked goods so wind doesn't blow it away. People will appreciate knowing what each item is. Also, consider labeling allergy items like "nuts", "milk" and "gluten", or simply label items that contain no allergens with "no nuts", "no milk", or "no gluten". Try to put foods that kids enjoy right up front where they can easily reach them and things that adults love towards the rear. Recipe cards can be included for free or ask for donations for recipe cards as well!

- Identify Volunteers – Wear shirts, aprons or vests so everyone looks alike, spread out so that you can catch a large audience. This does not need to be fancy or complicated; dress everyone in yellow or green. Clothes do not have to be a specific brand or even style, but if everyone has the same color of shirt, that is usually enough. There is always the option to create your own event t-shirts for a reasonable cost. Plain shirts in the same color can be purchased and printable iron on sheets can be used to add your own event logo. Fun shirts for kids groups can also be done with paints, brushes and hands. This way everyone can look exactly the same. The same iron-on pieces could be used for aprons or vests. Also a varied age, gender, and ethnicity of volunteers will help to appeal to a wider audience.
- Location – Consider locations outside of a mega-mart, sporting event, public attraction like a courthouse or park where you know that there may be a lot of people. Choose to sit in front of the busiest door or most heavily traveled path. If the location has more than one entrance consider placing a couple of volunteers with a sign in front of the secondary door.
- Baked Goods – Making a varied selection of baked goods and packaging them in a variety of quantities so that a single individual or a family can get a

package that meets their needs. It is a good idea to bake things that aren't sold often in that area. Consider items like fudge, pizzelles, pretzels, homemade fortune cookies, whoopee pies, éclairs, cream horns, fruit dumplings, dinner rolls, quick breads, and any other ethnic desert or delicacy that you love from your childhood but you can't find in stores. Most importantly have the old reliable baked goods as well; the never fail chocolate chip cookies and sugar cookies.

- Information – Volunteers are on hand to answer detailed questions about the organization, pamphlets are on hand about the organization as well as information about where the donated money goes. Fliers, brochures, stands, displays, flags, and all those other things you break out for special occasions. I have even seen some groups bring along radios. Just make sure that you can hear your customers over the music, and that your music selection does not include mature content (unless you are at a mature event).

So all of those details paint your big picture and what a person will be looking at when they turn to glance at your booth. What you are going for is a clean and approachable bake sale. The next time you walk past a store window, take a second and step back for the big picture. From a quick glance can you tell what they sell and does it draw you in? That same feeling should be present at your Bake Sale.

Key 2. Your Volunteers

Volunteers have to balance work, family, kids, housework, and life with their volunteer work. They do all of this with no financial compensation. Many of the people who run the volunteer coordination also do this with no financial compensation, so at times things can get hectic. In the end though, volunteers do some amazing things with a little help from their friends.

Start by planning your event in advance and having 1 or 2 people who will be completely responsible for bringing the donated food to the bake sale. Other volunteers can drop off their donations to those individuals the day or several days before (if they can be frozen) so that you can accommodate more people and get more bakers. This does not mean that you only have two people responsible for the whole bake sale, setting up, tearing down and all that jazz! This just means that you have two point people who will be responsible and make a solid effort to have all of the baked goods show up on time and in the right place.

If you have enough volunteers beyond the 2 for the baked goods, consider these additional positions: 1 responsible for setting up the tables the day of the event; 1 responsible for tearing down the tables at the end of the event; 1 responsible for making sure that everyone gets a bathroom break; 1 responsible for kids; 1 responsible for the money; 1 responsible for the garbage; 1 responsible for the volunteers. Depending on the number of volunteers that you can muster for your event, you may think up other jobs that I have mentioned throughout the book, but these are some great ones to start with.

Use the tools that the Internet has given you. There are apps out there that can help you coordinate across multiple platforms for folks who share schedules, things like Wunderlist, Google Calendar, Facebook and a whole host of others. Take advantage of your volunteers who utilize their devices daily and keep them connected through something that they are already using. Also, for the volunteers who are not online, have a call chain so that they are also reminded and kept in the loop. A call the day before the event, and again the morning of the event, just to be sure that your volunteers do not need any help and that they are all running on time can sometimes save the day.

It is a good idea if you also have a point person for the volunteers clothing, especially if you are having special shirts made or aprons/vests for the event. That way only one person brings the box of shirts/aprons/vests and they get handed out the day of the event to the people who show up. This way you don't have them **Missing In Action** when you need them most. Try to remember that every one of your volunteers has a busy schedule and the more planning that gets done before the event, the better chances of success.

Many of you will be selecting sales locations that have bathrooms for changing shirts, so bringing the shirts to the sale and having people run to the restroom to change may be an option. It may also be a way to handle volunteers who have forgotten to bring the right color shirt with them to the event. Keep extra shirts on hand so that if a volunteer shows up and forgets their shirt, an extra could be there to be thrown on. If each volunteer is asked to bring a second shirt along, or if shirts or aprons are made specially for the event, then there should be a number of extras on hand should a need arise.

If it is a group of folks who already have their own shirts, vests, or aprons like girl scouts or cheer leaders or veterans groups for example, it is a good idea for the person heading the whole event to have a few generic aprons made up that say "X Supporter" on the apron in case some friends or family show up and want to help. That way they can also be identified as volunteers and you will have some extra aprons for years to come. I say aprons, because they are the most versatile for various sizes or shapes of helpers. Some of the youth programs have "parent of" shirts, but not aunt, grandma, sibling shirts. So having the un-identified volunteer apron would fill that void.

Remember to acknowledge your helpers after the event is over, and to celebrate the work that they have done. If you are sending out a letter to the newspaper like I mentioned in the beginning, then consider mentioning your volunteers. If you are posting after the event on Social Media, then tag your volunteers or mention them by name. If anyone in particular was of key importance, then mention him or her by name and the specific job that they did. People need to know that their help meant a lot. This will encourage volunteers to continue helping with the cause and it will also encourage new individuals to volunteer.

By acknowledging your volunteers and helping them know that you appreciate them, they will tell their friends. As others see how much difference people are making, then they will want to be a part of that change too. It may only be that they want to make a donation, which is great, but they may want to volunteer and be a part of your group. A great volunteer organization is a family and the members take care of each other and have fun at their events. People are attracted to that, and will invite others into their family.

Key 3. The Location

Let us talk location and where you are going to set up your table. You have a lot of options here, and depending on your cause, location will make a big difference. The most important factors are listed here in order:

1. Time of Year
2. Space for Setup
3. Foot Traffic
4. Time Allowed to Display
5. Protection from Weather
6. Permission
7. Distance from your Volunteers

You have decided to do a bake sale so you need to first look at the time of year. How will you deal with the weather; is it hot, cold, rainy? What holidays are near? If you are doing it in the winter, then you will have to consider the comfort of your volunteers and the ability for your customers to stand in the cold to look at your wares. This may make an indoor location more appealing. On the other hand if you are looking to do a bake sale in the summer, and it is a bright shiny 90 degree day, you will need to look for cover for your bake sale or all of your items will sweat in your bags. It isn't very appealing to buy soggy buns or squishy cookies, and especially not cupcakes that have turned into melted puddles.

The space is important because if you have a great baking team and you need to setup 3 or 4 tables worth of displays, but the spot you have chosen will only allow you one, then you will not fit it all. Also, if a store or event provides you with a huge space and get very little baked goods you may have one successful sale, but the establishment may not let you back again. The best situation is to have 2-3 nice full tables with a few extra boxes underneath the table to replenish as the day goes on.

Foot traffic and time allowed to display go hand in hand with having permission. It is never a good idea to barge into a place and set up your goods and assume that the owner will have no trouble with you selling your treats outside of their store. It is safe to assume that the money a customer spends at your bake sale table, will not be spent inside the store, and even if they may not have spent that money in the store, the storeowner could believe that they would have.

Always ask permission first, and while you are asking permission, consider asking the owner which days and times they are the busiest. By knowing when the busiest days and times are for your chosen location, you will be able to put yourself in front of the most people. Some storeowners will ask for insurance forms or proof documenting what organization for whom you are fundraising. It is best to take this documentation with you when you approach the business manager or owner.

Look for locations with a single point of entry so that people will walk past you and not be able to avoid you by using the secondary entrance. If there is a second entrance to the location that you want to use; try to have two extra volunteers to man that second entrance. One of these volunteers should be holding a sign on average 2 feet by 3 feet the other should be holding a donation can. These volunteers should try to prompt people to head towards your bake sale, but let them know that you are accepting donations. Always remember to smile and when people say no, continue to smile; there will be someone else to talk to. Others are watching you and if you respond positively they may come over to make a donation.

Encourage your volunteers to suggest locations that are familiar to them. If the locations you choose for your bake sale are too far from where your volunteers work or live, it will be difficult for you to get good participation. The volunteers are donating a significant amount of time and money to this cause and to ask for an even greater investment by having them travel may prevent participation not only in this event but in future events.

Key 4. The Display

As we have talked about so far, the display is what will make or break your sales. Good looking food, in good looking packages, on a good-looking table sold by happy volunteers. Dare I say it again; you are the big picture. So, how can we improve the picture and what steps can we take to improve sales.

The Sign

The sign is the first thing that someone approaching your bake sale should see. Think big chunky letters and bright colors. A computer-designed poster may look like this:

Bake Sale

To Benefit Your Quality Cause

Your donations will be going towards helping pay for _____ in _____.
The building for this effort starts on _____. Thank you for your help!

Cash Donations for Baked Goods. Minimum of $1 donation per item please.

You can easily copy this same language onto a hand painted or drawn poster. Insert your own event information into the blank sections and your cause name into the "X Quality Cause".

There are several materials that are inexpensive and readily available that can be great for producing signs. One material that I frequently use is a plastic tablecloth because they are often less than $4 each and can be found in a wide assortment of colors. Another option is fabric, which can also be attained from the discount bin; often less than $3/yard. Either of these options works well for hand painted or drawn signs. Some other materials to consider for making your own banners are wrapping paper, meat packing paper, poster paper, art paper and shower curtains. I have seen fabric scraps, old curtains and bed sheets at garage or yard sales as well for very low prices, so if you bake sale watch these locations for sign materials.

There are many stores that will print posters and banners if your bake sale is an annual or semi-annual event, or if you would like a more professional look. Occasionally printers will make donations or discounts to quality causes. It never hurts to ask! If you work with multiple locations and do lots of bake sales each year, making a generic bake sale sign and having it printed at one of these locations may be a money/time saving option. Purchasing iron on lettering or glue on felt lettering is also an option for those individuals and groups who aren't feeling the painting/drawing bug. Printing out your own lettering and cutting it out is also a fun option for groups with younger children and a way to get them involved in sign making. Taping together printed sheets of paper is also another way to make larger signs.

The Tables

Each table needs to be clean and should not shake or wobble. Tables can be store bought or made, and I have encountered various locations that offered up the use of their personal tables. It is always best to ask the location if they have tables/chairs that you could use when you solicit for the date of your bake sale. It is also a good idea to have a table or two as backup just in case. The actual configuration of the tables is a little more challenging.

One Table - This is the easiest configuration to manage, however it depends on the setup of your background how you will manage arranging this table in association to its surroundings for best interaction with the crowd. When it is just the table and a wall, the only real option is to line the table up with the wall or angle it slightly so that you are not endangering the flow of traffic for either the people or the vehicles.

For a single table in the corner, you may want to angle it so that no one can get around you and access the back of the table where your volunteers are, chairs and money are located.

However if the doors for the entrance are off to one side it would be better to adjust the angle of the table so that it faces the doors.

For a single table along a wall with a door, you will need to assess the direction of the parking lot to the door and the way that the guests walk as the exit the door. The arrow in this case points towards the door, and the table is angled towards the parking lot with the wall to its back.

This way the patrons can see the goods as they walk in and the volunteers can talk to the guests as they walk out. If the table where at a 90 degree angle with the wall, it would be difficult to see from the parking lot and the volunteers would have to do a lot more work to interact with the patrons.

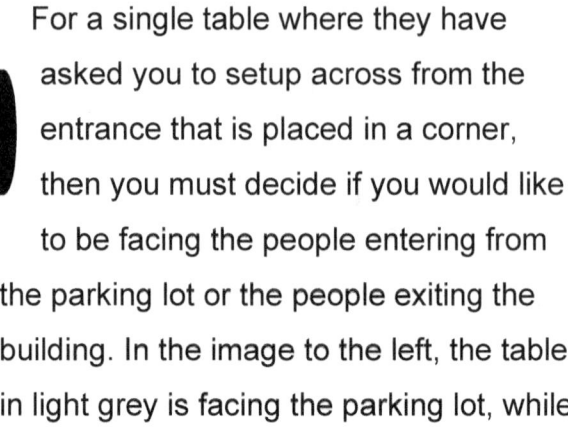

For a single table where they have asked you to setup across from the entrance that is placed in a corner, then you must decide if you would like to be facing the people entering from the parking lot or the people exiting the building. In the image to the left, the table in light grey is facing the parking lot, while the black table is facing the door to the right represented by the black oval. At the light grey table, you are facing the parking lot people will see you as they are walking in towards the building and that can be nice if you are mostly collecting donations, however people generally do not carry items into a store with them. The black table, you are facing the door, you can catch people's attention as they are leaving the store. While you may miss some of the viewing from the parking lot, you will be catching all of their attention as they leave.

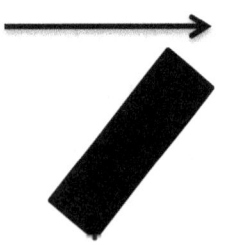

Now do NOT GET TRAPPED! Some people will say to themselves "I will turn my table sideways here just like in the corner". This makes your table a funnel to channel people right out of the store, past you and into the parking lot. Most people have already made their planned purchases and are on the way to their car, so you need to be in their direct line of sight to be a visual distraction.

For Multiple Tables

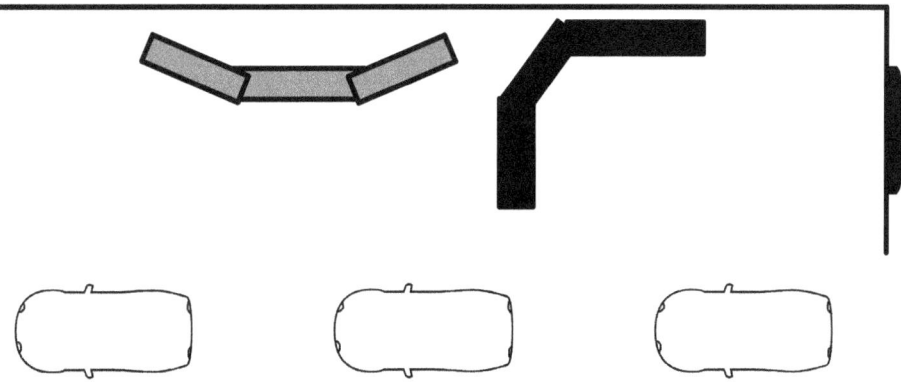

Here are two examples of multiple table setups that could be used. The all black tables are set up like a funnel or buffet line and this setup is best when you need to have a display from two different directions. With this design it will be necessary to have two signs, one from each end table. The best would be to have them in the air above each end table. The second example shown in light grey set of tables that is setup in an arch. The arch can be setup against a wall. It is designed to give a large area for the crowd to view the baked goods and a smaller area for the volunteers to maintain control of the sale. A larger single sign is great for this second design. Either design works well under a tent.

Key 5. Food

Food is a fun topic to talk about and the key component to a bake sale. The food component of the bake sale is the one least planned and the part that makes or breaks the sale. Bake sales do not always have to be sweet and they do not always have to be cookies. What they do have to be is portable and packaged so that people can carry them. Packaged for safe and convenient transportation. Make sure that liquids cannot leak and that bags are sealed. They also have to be in manageable sizes, and portions that meet consumer needs so that you can sell them.

It is always good to check your state law if you want to sell items like hot foods, drinks, or candies. These sorts of things are not always covered for sale in every location. This includes food that is not prepackaged when it arrives at the bake sale. It is also not safe to assume that you will be permitted to sell items that are cooked or prepared on site. Foods such as these may fall under restrictions that require certain permissions, which may include food handling restrictions. With the correct forms in place however, things like hotdogs, hamburgers, coffee, hot cocoa, and much more can be added to a bake sale to increase revenue.

I have often been to bake sales where people will bake full 9"x13" cakes thinking that people will give $20-$30 donations for these cakes. This is appropriate for a beautiful bakery style cake, on in quality box, with great ingredients and a designer icing job. However, don't expect to get that kind of donation from a box mix cake, in a disposable pan, with canned icing.

I decided to bake goods that were not regularly offered at stores nearby. I made chocolate fudge, monster cream puffs and peanut butter cookies. The cream puffs didn't last the first half hour. At this particular sales we took donations only, we got anywhere from $5/$10 per cream puff. My cost to make the cream puffs was $16 for all 20. Almost everyone who bought one stood there and ate it right on the spot and several of the folks bought a second. The fudge was bagged in ¼ pound bricks and donations were $10-$20 per brick and it was also gone very quickly. The peanut butter cookies were hit and miss, some folks loved them and some just looked at them.

If you have experienced bakers consider asking them to bake some things that are not seen in the store every day. Ask them for old family favorites, things they bake only for the holidays, mini loaves of quick breads. Consider baking things that people always wish that they had, but that stores do not bake, think along the lines of banana bread and miniature apple pies. All of these things that are made from fresh ingredients that are generally not found other than at high end restaurants or bakeries. Here is my list of go to items: Apple dumplings; chocolate chip cookies; peanut butter cookies; candied apples; chocolate covered pretzels; popcorn balls; fudge; peanut butter cookies; cake pops; pepperoni rolls; éclairs; bread; zucchini bread; carrot cake; chocolate cake; vanilla cake; cupcakes baked in ice cream cones; soft pretzels; chocolate covered marshmallows on a stick rolled in sprinkles; chocolate covered everything; fried donuts; cake donuts; and just about anything on the Food Network!

For your non-experienced bakers, who still want to participate, but are only able to work with out of the box recipes. Consider asking them to bake non-sweet recipes that are still cost effective. Frozen bread can be turned into pepperoni rolls very effectively and the cost to make 18 rolls is less than $20. It only requires 3 loaves of frozen bread, 1 stick of pepperoni, and 1 pound of very thinly sliced provolone. Each loaf of bread is defrosted and raised by half and then sliced into 6. Work each section out into a flat rectangle and then place sliced pepperoni and thinly sliced cheese in the middle, start from the edge closest to you and roll tightly to the other side. Then pinch it off. Bake the finished rolls on a cookie sheet covered in parchment paper; do not raise, bake at time and temperature noted on the bread package.

Pepperoni rolls are a great addition to any bake sale, and they taste great hot or cold. They sell very well in many areas, and if they are a new item for your market, people who love pizza take to them quickly. Instead of pepperoni rolls the bread dough can also be stuffed with cheese and spinach, or broccoli. Another favorite treat is bread dough made sweet with butter, cinnamon and sugar. This way you can encourage your non-experienced bakers to do more then just buy the "break and bake" cookies from the store. This will grow the offerings at the bake sale and boost the confidence of your volunteers.

Key 6. The Money

The light at the end of the tunnel, the golden ticket, the big bucks! Before your bake sale you must decide how you will collect your money. Will this be a per-item bake sale, a donation bake sale or a combination. If you do not already know what these mean, let me break it down.

Per-Item Bake Sale – Each item in the bake sale is marked with an individual price that is non-negotiable. For example: 4 cookies are $1, 2 cupcakes is $1, 4 brownies are $2.50

Donation Bake Sale – No item has a set price, buyers are allowed to take any item for any donation. Most of these types of bake sales set a minimum donation amount. For example: Minimum donation $1 for any item, cookies are in packs of 4, cupcakes in packs of 2, brownies in packs of 2 ect…

Combination Bake Sale – This is a bake sale combined of mixed and set prices. Usually it will have smaller items with set prices like the cookies and cupcakes from the per-item example above, but then it may have larger fancy items. I have seen where local area bakeries have donated items costing upwards of $60-$100 if purchased, these items are then given away for donations in kind. Often bringing in a donations of $50 - $100, with the volunteers asking a minimum donation of $40.

Once you decide which kind of bake sale you want to have then it is time to determine how to handle the cash. Another thing to decide if you are going to have a per-item bake sale is if you want to handle coins, and how much change minimum you need to have on hand. Also, if you are having a bake sale on the weekend or in the evening, there will be no way for you to get change if you run out. For the per-item bake sale, you will need to have change on hand and a money box. Remember that people often carry larger bills, and that if they are getting cash back at the stores it will probably be larger bills as well. It will also be important to have a calculator on hand in case you have a customer who is purchasing multiple items. It will be important for your volunteers to understand how to properly make change and to know that they should always keep the buyers money out of the cash drawer until the change has been accepted. This way there can be no argument that the buyer actually gave the volunteer a $20 bill when it was in fact a $10 bill that was given. As wrong as it is, some people will try to take advantage others even though it is for a worthy cause. Other change tips: Count back the change starting with how much they spent and then go up from there until you reach the original amount submitted for payment; coins first, then small bills to large bills; try to keep your bills facing the same way in the box; try to separate your bills in the box; only keep a set amount in the box and store the rest in a safe alternate place.

For the donation bake sale, consider have several donation containers so that when one gets full; it can be changed out and/or emptied. I love to use empty oatmeal containers with printed donation information on 8 ½" x 11" papers and cut to fit, and attached to the outside of the container. A hole for the money can be easily cut into the lid for donations. If you have enough oatmeal containers then you can tape the lids shut and put the containers away as they fill so that no one knows how much money you have collected. Any container with a sound base that you cannot see through would make a logical choice.

Some groups with whom I have volunteered have even used large barrels as their donation buckets so that they were too heavy to be stolen. While this seems like a great idea, it made it hard for more than one person to donate at a time. Also, with multiple donation containers, if one does get stolen, then all of the money isn't gone. Remember to place trusted volunteers near each donation receptacle for that very reason. Never place a child alone with a donation container if something were to happen, it isn't fair or safe for the child.

Chapter 4. The Marketing Nut

You have read this far, so now you are here in the world of the marketing nut. Like me you may have asked yourself how some groups sell out their bake sale in an hour and others sit there all day with the best snacks in the world. Heck, some of them can sit in the exact same location. But here is a clue… it is at a different time of day, on a different day of the week, and a different time of the year. One more clue, the organizations are different kinds of organizations with different social media presences.

Social Media

Lets talk about social media for a moment shall we. Consider the generational difference between a group of women in their 60's who do not actively use social media (Group A) and a group of girls in their teens who live on social media (Group B). What are the chances that Group A are on Facebook, Twitter, Instagram or any of those other social media sites? Chances are maybe for Facebook, but pretty rare for any of the other Social Media sites and it is highly unlikely that they are on there multiple times a day with hundreds of local friends that they chat with constantly. We can't say the same about Group B, they are probably on most if not all of those sites and probably multiple times a day.

If Group A and Group B are going to have a bake sale for the same reason and on the same day, but at 2 different locations then how are they most likely going to advertise. Chances are Group A will simply set up their table at a location that has worked well for them before and set up a nice table with a little sign. Group B will blast all of their friends days before, they will Tweet, Facebook, and Instagram pictures of themselves at the table, telling everyone where they are and how long they will be there. Group B will make sure that the world knows what they are doing. Will Group B outsell Group A, maybe or maybe not. It is highly likely that more people will know about Group B's cause and their event because of their use of Social Media.

Ways to take advantage of Social Media

- Take pictures as you are setting up your bake sale and post those pictures to every "BUY/SWAP/SELL" page for that community that the site is located in along with the bake sale dates and times
- Take a picture of every volunteer in front of the bake sale table and post it on their timeline with the times for the bake sale. Have them tag every one of their local friends. Each volunteer as well as the group should post in order to improve the awareness.
- Instragram pictures every time you sell out of something or if there are only a few left of something

that is a big seller. Make people feel like they are missing out.

- Post anonymous donations over $50 and if the people want their pictures on your page with their donations, put them there. Invite others to come on down and make their donations as well.

Ethnic Foods

People forget sometimes that there are areas and people living in communities that do not get to eat ethnic food that they love. For example pizzelles, I have been surprised at how many places that I have lived or visited where people had never eaten or seen a pizzelles. I made pizzelles for one of my bake sales and every person that came up to the table asked what they were. We sold all 200 that I made and every person that tried them there was very happy. It is a very inexpensive cookie to make, and it takes just a little practice and time. So when you or your volunteers are considering baking for your bake sales consider your own ethnic backgrounds. Also consider those of your community. What types of restaurants are close by, then look at what types of restaurants are within an hour drive, a two-hour drive, a three-hour drive. Look for a pattern or a lack of pattern.

If you see a considerable lack of Italian restaurants then perhaps look up some Italian cookie recipes, pepperonis roll recipes, cannoli. This will be new to people and they may be willing to pay a little bit more for something different. What if you see an overwhelming number of fast food restaurants, then perhaps the simple sugar cookie or the butter cookie is a bad idea

Likewise, you need to check out the local grocery stores. What kind of baked goods do they sell and at what price? What do they look like? If they have boxes of a dozen chocolate chip cookies for $3 and they are large and pretty good looking and then you are outside trying to sell 4 small cookies for $1, that look like they came out of the "break and bake" section …… well. You need to know the competition and understand what the consumer will be interested in. If the local grocery store is your bake sale's location (why would you do that to yourself!) then try to bake things that they don't have.

Location

There is so much more about a location then just the location. Think about what the location sells and how your bake sale will compliment what is going on there. Ask yourself these questions when you are trying to pick your location.

- Do people buy food here?
- Do people leave this location with their arms full?
- Do people bring children to this location?

- Do people leave this location hungry?
- Do people come this location with cash?

Let's ponder that first question for a minute. **Do people buy food here?** This is important for a couple of reasons. The first reason is that if it is a store like a grocery store where people are shopping for staples and food for meals, they likely have a list of items to buy and unless they are really swayed by your cause or what is on your table, they probably won't be buying from you. In fact they have the opportunity to price shop and compare what is on your table to the ingredients of what is inside the store. This could be dangerous.

If it is for donation sales, you may get lower donations because whether they realize it or not people have devalued your products. They may forget that your efforts have value, as they price the ingredients for the item on the table. If it is for price sales, then they are looking at the cookie and saying $3 a dozen that I make myself and $1 for 4 cookies at the bake sale. They may be thinking, "Nope, I will take the break and bakes home and have fresh hot cookies from the oven." While you will win some of the time, you are giving people the excuse to purchase the items in the store with the credit card instead of buying it with cash from you.

Do people leave this location with their arms full? If this is a store that doesn't have buggies for it's shoppers, but it gets a lot of shoppers and it sells a bunch of stuff, how do they carry it all. I have been to a few stores where the customers came out with their arms loaded down with bags and boxes of stuff and while it seemed like it could have been a great location for a bake sale, there was no way the people could have picked up any baked goods. So even though it was busy it just wouldn't have worked. Some hardware centers are like this because even though they have buggies, the people are so busy balancing wood and hardware that they would loose their purchases trying to find their wallet.

Do people bring children to this location? We all know that parents want to be in control of their children, but when it comes to a $1 bag of cookies most of the time the children win. So if you are looking at 2 locations and one is frequented with people with children, and the other is not child friendly, it is probably a better bet to pick first. It is also a better bet that the parents have a dollar or two worth of change in their pocket. They pick it up here or there. They used it for this and had some left over.

Do people leave this location hungry? Think about some of the places in your life where you leave hungry. I remember as a little kid when I went to school and I would leave famished! School bake sales can be held at football games or during after school functions. All of these times are great because the kids are ready to eat and parents are just coming off of work.

I know that when I worked with some churches they started offering lunch for their parishioners because they were hungry after service. Youth groups will occasionally have bake sales to help fund their events and they would hold those during the lunches offered by the churches. The youth would make the deserts being offered that day. Other churches would hold bake sales after services or during their yard sale fundraisers.

What other times are attractive for bake sales? It has been my experience that the day before a big game is an excellent day for a bake sale in front of mega stores that sell game day "stuff". If game day falls on a Sunday and you can get your bake sale on game day at the super center between 10am – 4pm when the churches let out and before the game begins, this is also a very good time. Remember though that if the super center sells groceries, you will be competing with them and this can lower your sales. It is a win/loose scenario.

Do people come here with cash? The cash question is a biggie! Not every group has a dedicated checking account, but if you do and are able, then you should consider PayPal or Square. This will enable you to counter the "I only have credit cards" comments. The first way to avoid "I only have credit cards" is to look for locations where people generally take cash. Most people do not purchase living room furniture with cash, so going to the high priced furniture store (even though it is hopping) may not be the premium option for your bake sale. The same is true for the local gas station. You may have the biggest gas station in a 30 mile radius that does business 24/7, hundreds of cars a day, but most people probably pay at the pump.

Other cashless considerations are more based on days. Consider when individuals are more likely to get paid. It is typically not the end of the month. Also, paydays are often on Fridays, and Saturdays. Mondays through Thursdays are typically bad days for money. Look to the largest employers in your community and try to identify which days of the month they pay on.

Location Analysis

Now you have determined a location and asked yourself the important questions about it. It is time to talk to the owner of the establishment. If the owner is willing to let you have your bake sale at anytime, ask if they know their busiest days and times. If they do not know this information then ask if you can get back to him/her in a week with the date of your bake sale. Here are the things you need to analyze about the location. First narrow down possible days of the week for your volunteers to work the bake sale with you. Doing some recon work will help you establish the best use of your time. This chart can guide you. Make the chart below on a piece of scrap paper adjusting for your times.

Saturday	9am	10am	11am	12pm	1pm	2pm	3pm	4pm	5pm	6pm
Cars										
Adults										
Children										
Seniors										

Tracking the activity at your chosen business on this chart will help determine the best times. If you are considering several locations, it does not hurt to have a volunteer sit in the parking lot and keep track of the people coming and going, and one person does not have to keep track of the whole day. You can have volunteers count in two-hour increments or if you know that you have two sections of time you are considering, then have one volunteer watch one segment of time and have another volunteer watch the other.

Accounting

Yes, I said it, do not laugh! If at all possible make a list of who baked what for each bake sale and how much of each item was provided. Then at the end of the bake sale make a list of how much was left of each. Also make special notes if something sold particularly well, or if there were negative comments. Like my cream puffs from the example earlier, it is important to note if you have a volunteer who's items are highly demanded. It is also necessary to note if it is the item that was in demand, or if it was the location that made the difference. Let me help explain with a scenario.

Bake sale A:

Volunteer H – 10 mini apple pies, Volunteer T – 10 bags of 4 Donuts, Volunteer U – 10 bags of Chocolate Chip Cookies Bake Sale is outside of a Mega Mart that does not sell food and the sale is from 10am – Noon. Sells out of Donuts in the first half hour, left with 2 pies and 1 bag of chocolate chip cookies. Total for the day $65.

Bake sale B:

Volunteer H – 10 mini apple pies, Volunteer T – 10 bags of 4 Donuts, Volunteer U – 10 bags of Chocolate Chip Cookies Bake Sale is outside of a Mega Mart that does not sell food and the sale is from 2pm – 5pm. Sells out of cookies first half hour, left with 5 bags of donuts and no pies. Total for the day $95.

If you only had the first example to look at, then you would think that you needed Volunteer T to make donuts every bake sale, and if you only had the second example to look at then you would think that you needed Volunteer U to make Chocolate Chip Cookies every time. What you really need to look at is the culmination of the two examples and discover that the time of day in conjunction with the location is what makes the difference. In the first instance the shoppers where still looking for breakfast and so the donuts filled that need. In the second instance the shoppers where looking for a quick snack.

What is noteworthy is that the pies almost sold out both times, no matter what time of day, and that means that shoppers in this area clearly want apple pie no matter what. This means that no matter what time of day the bake sale happens as long as it is at the Mega Mart, Volunteer H should be asked to bake mini apple pies. Without accounting, it is possible that no one would have known this bit of information. Things like type of cookie, type of donut, special requests, all of that matters.

Routine Efforts

It does not have to be a single time effort. If you have the volunteer backing and the ability to get the bakers behind you, then consider scheduling regular bake sales, especially if you have a good location. Not every week, but quarterly or bi-annually can really help people know when to look for you. Think back to what I said about the Social Media for a second and consider if you have a page for your bake sales and people are linking to it, liking it, and talking about the amazing food that they bought from you. All the sudden, your small cause is a much larger cause and it is moving mountains.

Creating a Social Media presence you make a way for people to get ahold of you regularly through out the year and to make donations more often. It also opens up the doors for sponsorships from bakeries and restaurants. If you are able to advertise your supporters online, this makes them more likely to want to back you. What this can do for your bake sale is give you foods that you otherwise would have had to pay for out of pocket.

Sponsorships

You have established your good cause and you have broadcast it to the world. If you are a non-profit or not-for-profit and have the tax status to back it (or if you do not) let's talk about getting baked goods from non-volunteers. Once you know when and where your bake sale is and have established how you will be marketing your bake sale, you can approach contributors. You will also have to come with an established flier stating when the bake sale is. Have an idea of what you want from the people you are approaching, but most important know the cost of what they produce. Do not go into a store that makes $80 cakes and ask for 10 cakes or a $50 donation. The two just don't equal each other.

Some successful examples are for restaurants that sell things like cookies at $10 per dozen or small cakes for $10 each. At either of these locations I would ask for 2 – 4 dozen cookies, or 2-4 cakes, or $40 cash, or enough disposable containers for 100 servings. What this allows for is food for the bake sale or money to buy ingredients or containers to put baked goods in. In exchange we would place the businesses name on all of our signs and put a poster up for them on the table as well as put them on all of the Social Media content.

www.ingramcontent.com/pod-product-compliance
Lightning Source LLC
Chambersburg PA
CBHW071257280526
45788CB00004B/1745